Doeden, Matt.
John Sutter

W9-BNR-927

GRAPHIC LIBRARY

GRAPHIC HISTORY

JOHN SUTTER ★AND THE★ CALIFORNIA GOLD RUSH

by Matt Doeden

illustrated by Ron Frenz
and Charles Barnett III

Consultant:
John Mark Lambertson
Director and Archivist
National Frontier Trails Museum
Independence, Missouri

Capstone press
Mankato, Minnesota

Graphic Library is published by Capstone Press,
151 Good Counsel Drive, P.O. Box 669, Mankato, Minnesota 56002.
www.capstonepress.com

Copyright © 2006 by Capstone Press. All rights reserved.
No part of this publication may be reproduced in whole or in part, or stored in a
retrieval system, or transmitted in any form or by any means, electronic, mechanical,
photocopying, recording, or otherwise, without written permission of the publisher.
For information regarding permission, write to Capstone Press, 151 Good Counsel Drive,
P.O. Box 669, Dept. R, Mankato, Minnesota 56002.
Printed in the United States of America

1 2 3 4 5 6 10 09 08 07 06 05

Library of Congress Cataloging-in-Publication Data
Doeden, Matt.
    John Sutter and the California gold rush / by Matt Doeden; illustrated by Ron Frenz and
Charles Barnett, III.
    p. cm.—(Graphic library. Graphic history)
    Summary: In graphic novel format, tells the story of the discovery of gold at John Sutter's
mill and how it changed California.
    Includes bibliographical references and index.
    ISBN 0-7368-4370-1 (hardcover)
    1. California—Gold discoveries—Juvenile literature. 2. Sutter, John Augustus, 1803–1880—
Juvenile literature. I. Barnett, Charles, III ill. II. Frenz, Ron ill. III. Title. IV. Series.
F865.D63 2006
979.4'04—dc22   2005007890

Art and Editorial Direction
Jason Knudson and Blake A. Hoena

Designers
Bob Lentz and Kate Opseth

Colorist
Ben Hunzeker

Editor
Christopher Harbo

Editor's note: Direct quotations from primary sources are indicated by a yellow background.

Direct quotations appear on the following pages:
Page 6, from *Gold Dust and Gunsmoke: Tales of Gold Rush Outlaws, Gunfighters, Lawmen,
    and Vigilantes* by John Boessenecker (New York: John Wiley, 1999).
Page 27, from "The Discovery of Gold in California" by General John Sutter, *Hutchings'
    California Magazine*, 1857 (http://www.sfmuseum.org/hist2/gold.html).

TABLE OF CONTENTS

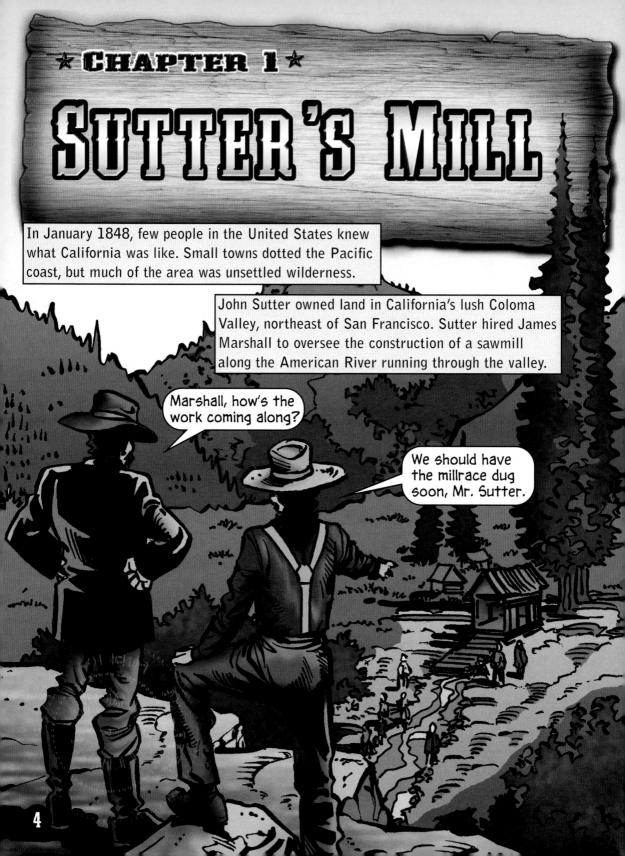

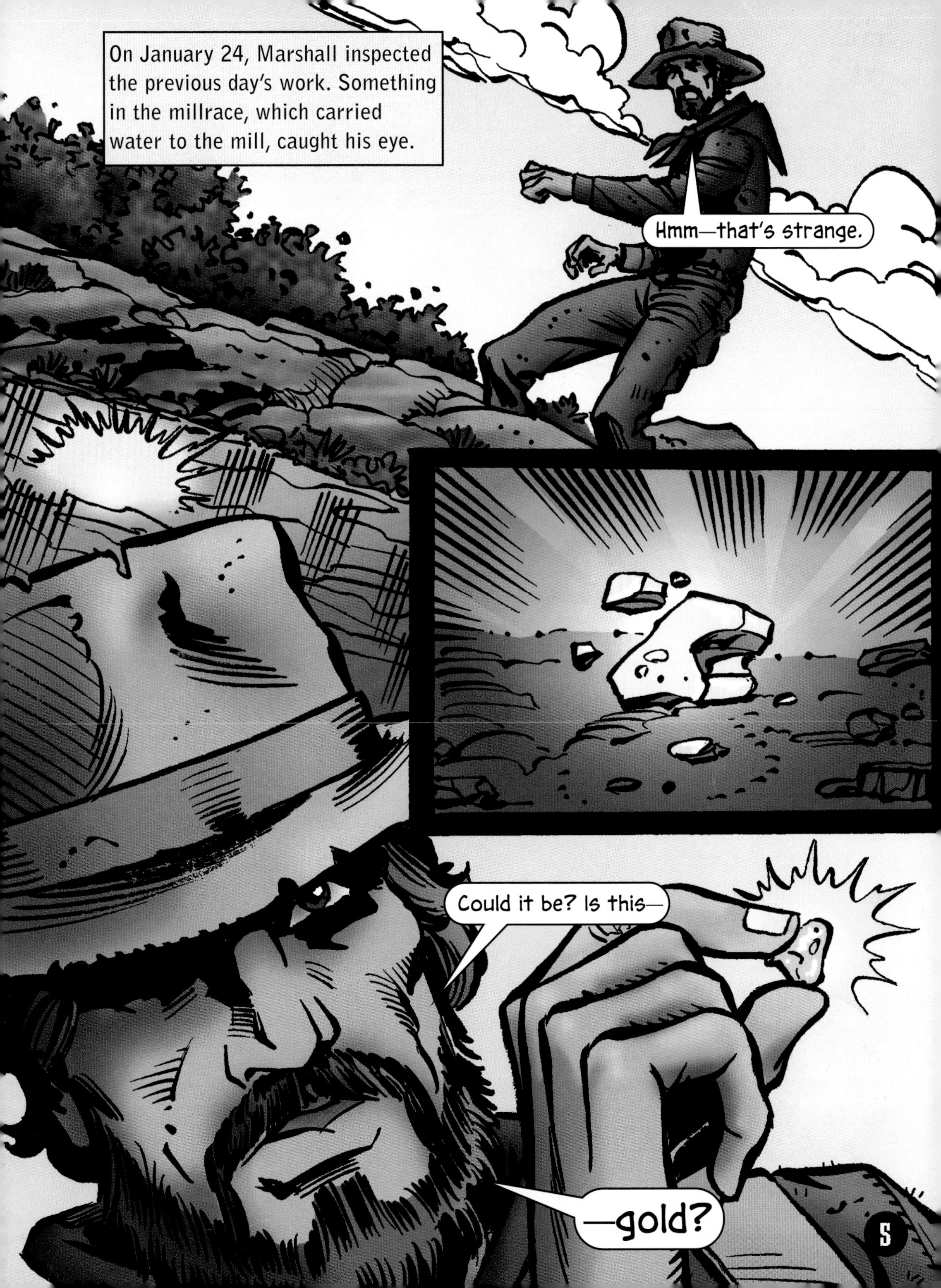
On January 24, Marshall inspected the previous day's work. Something in the millrace, which carried water to the mill, caught his eye.
Hmm—that's strange.
Could it be? Is this—
—gold?

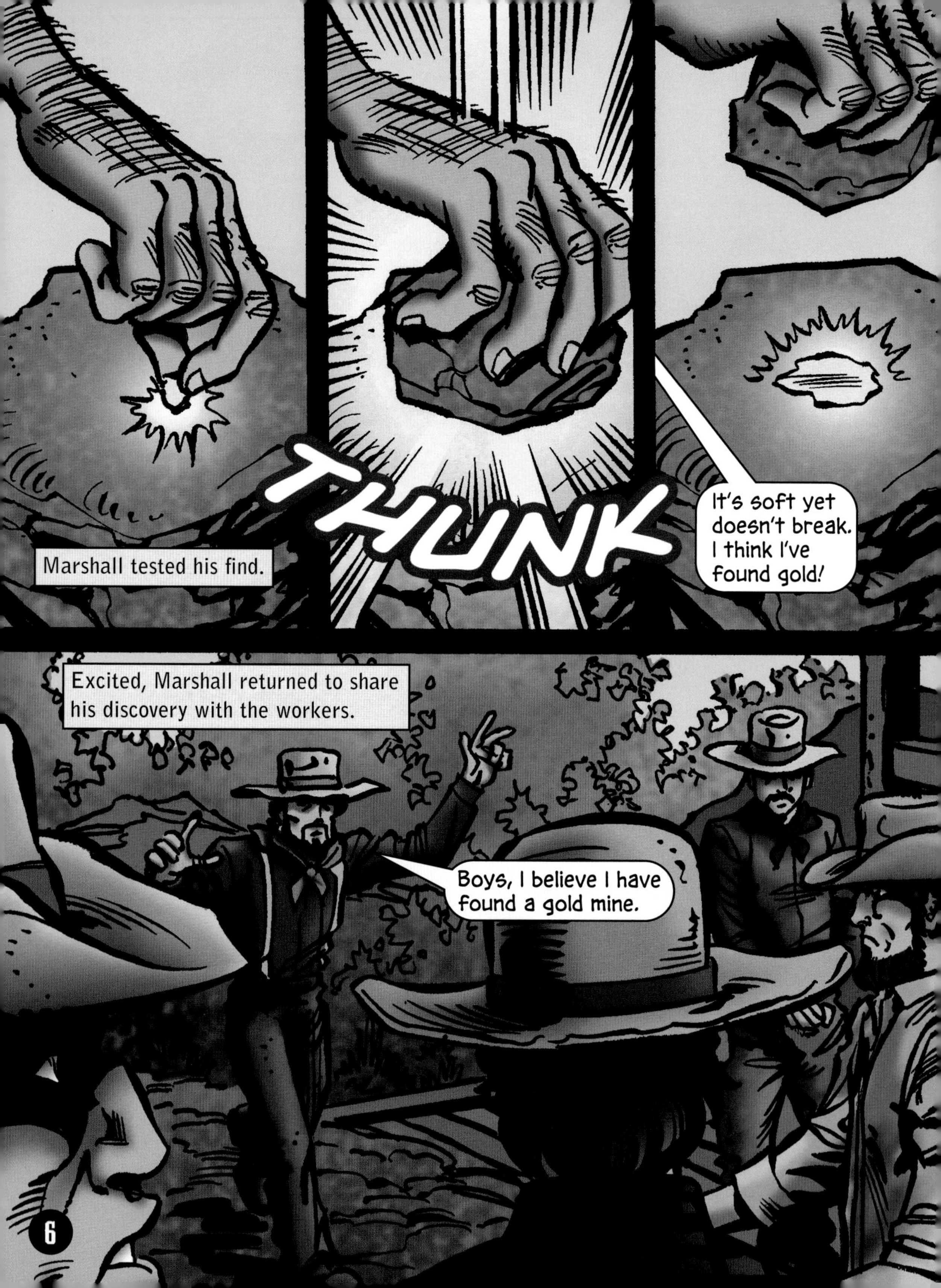
Marshall tested his find.
THUNK
It's soft yet doesn't break. I think I've found gold!
Excited, Marshall returned to share his discovery with the workers.
Boys, I believe I have found a gold mine.

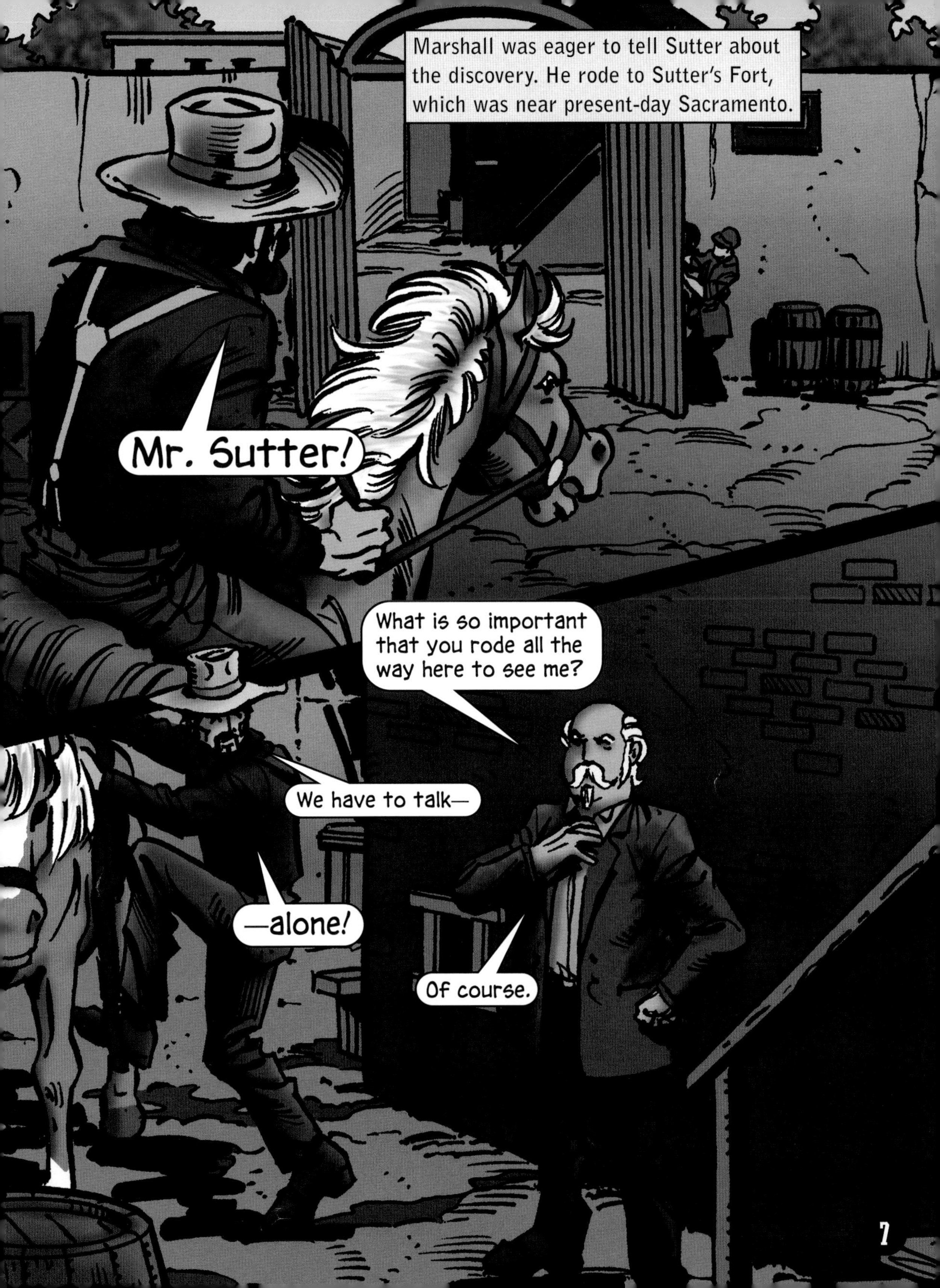
Marshall was eager to tell Sutter about the discovery. He rode to Sutter's Fort, which was near present-day Sacramento.
Mr. Sutter!
What is so important that you rode all the way here to see me?
We have to talk—
—alone!
Of course.

Chapter 2

The Secret Is Out

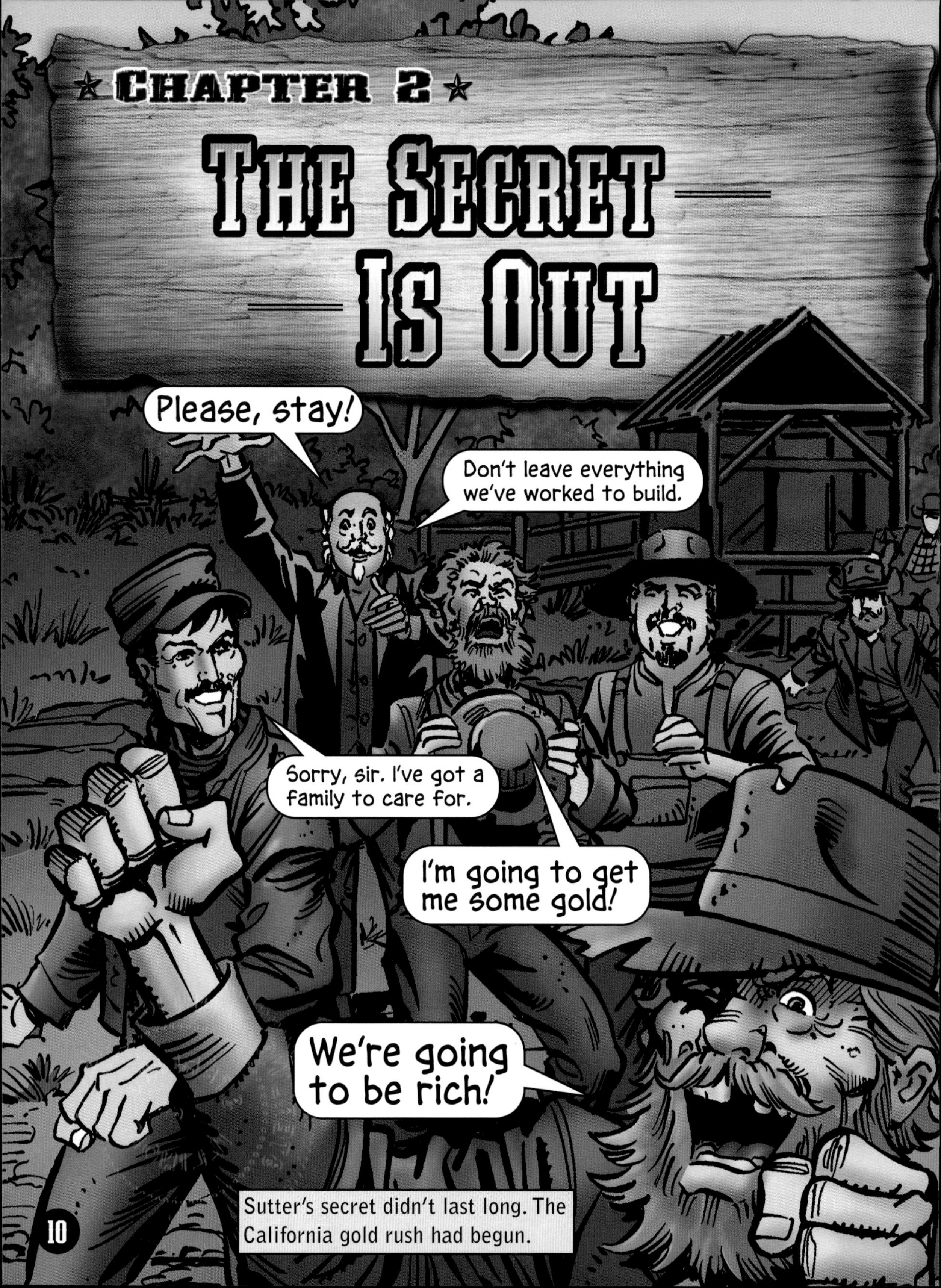
Please, stay!
Don't leave everything we've worked to build.
Sorry, sir. I've got a family to care for.
I'm going to get me some gold!
We're going to be rich!
Sutter's secret didn't last long. The California gold rush had begun.

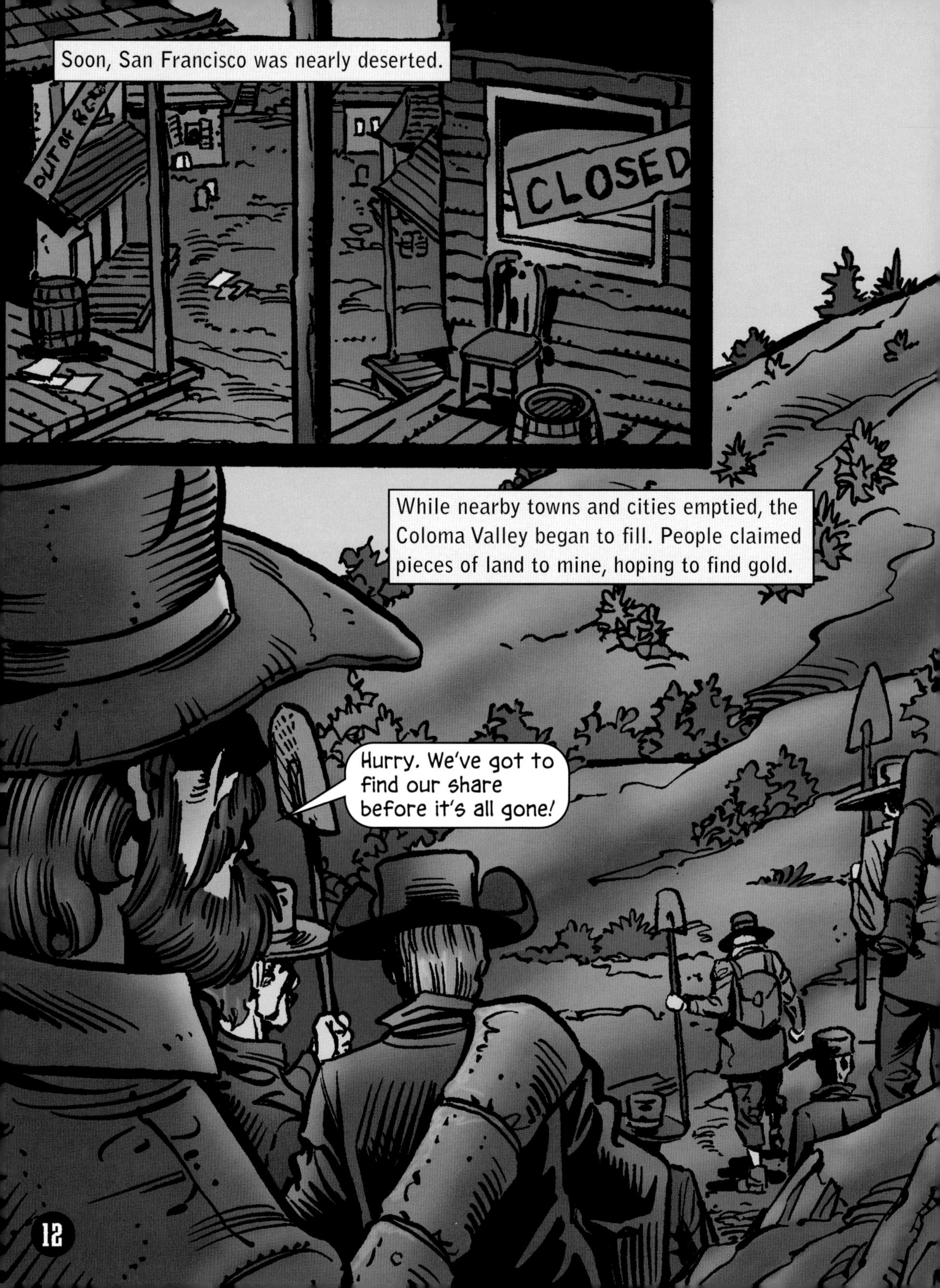
Soon, San Francisco was nearly deserted.
OUT OF R...
CLOSED
While nearby towns and cities emptied, the Coloma Valley began to fill. People claimed pieces of land to mine, hoping to find gold.
Hurry. We've got to find our share before it's all gone!

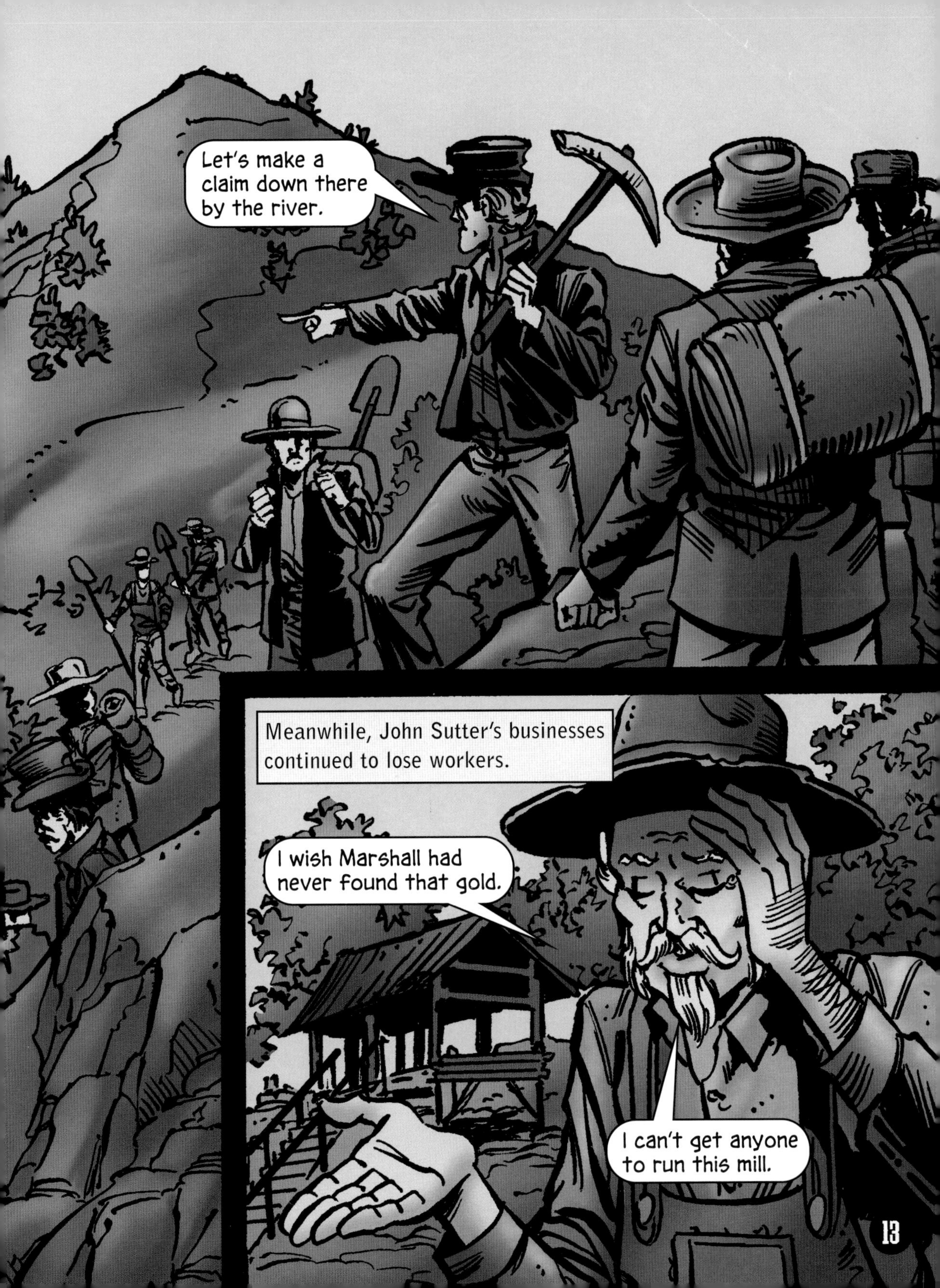
Let's make a claim down there by the river.
Meanwhile, John Sutter's businesses continued to lose workers.
I wish Marshall had never found that gold.
I can't get anyone to run this mill.

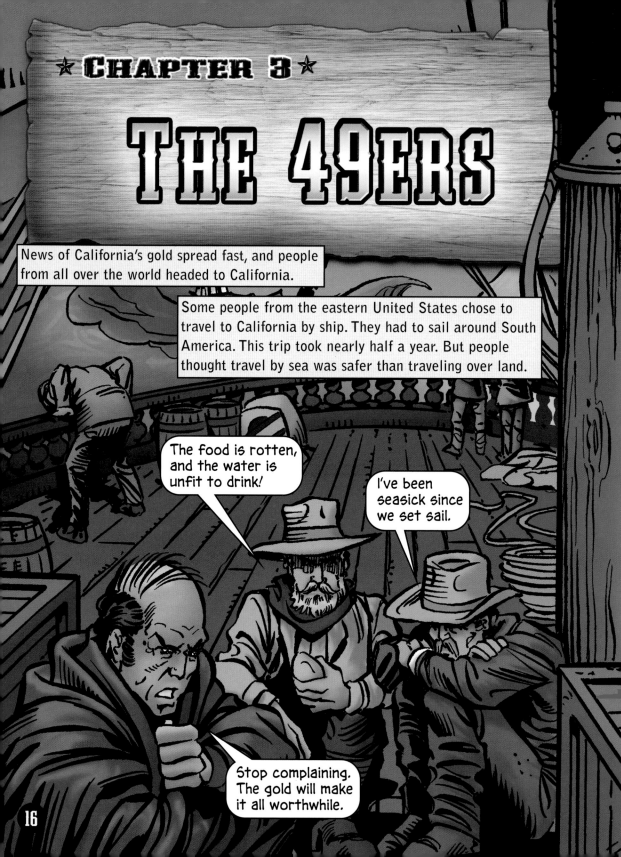

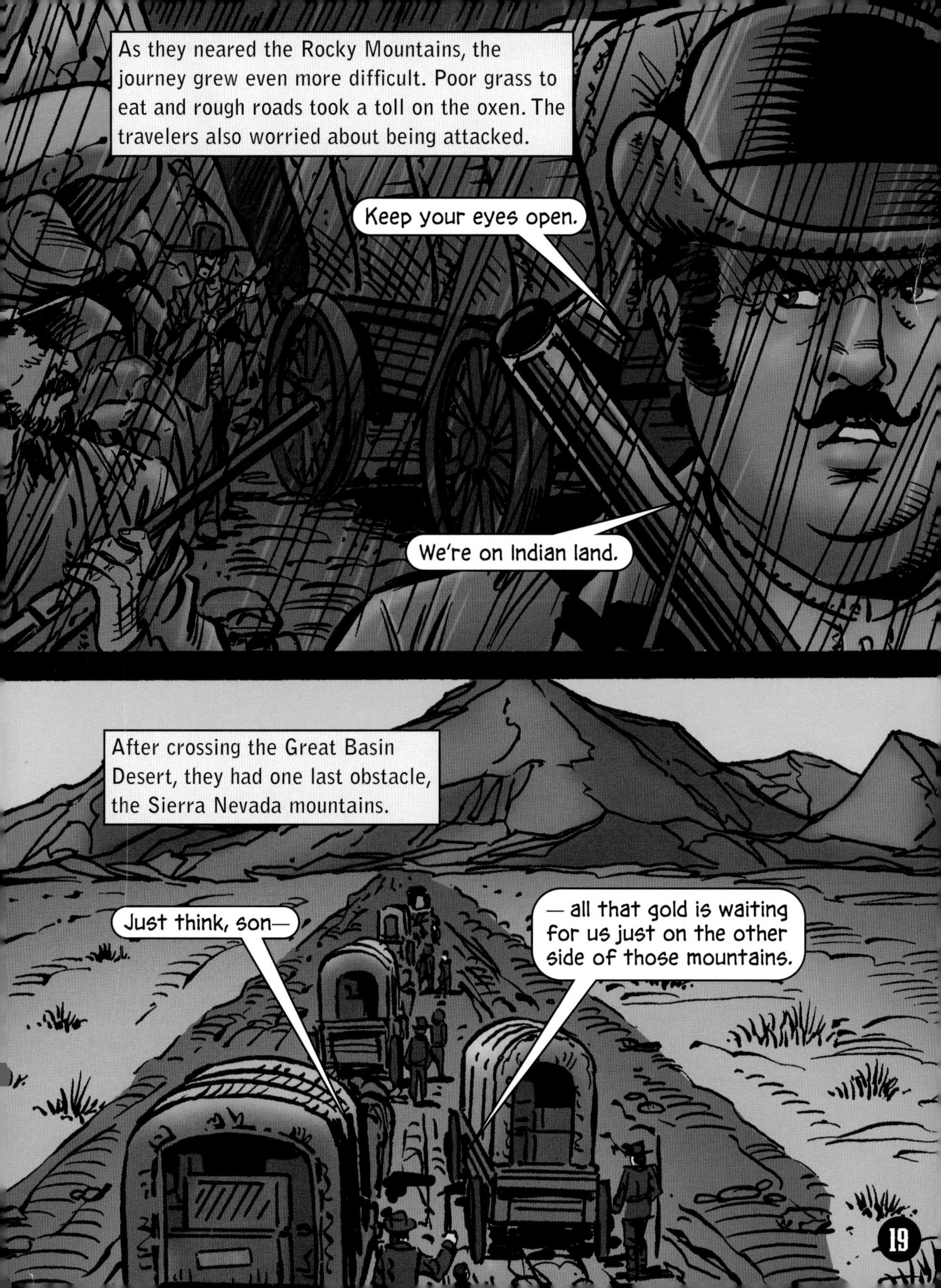
As they neared the Rocky Mountains, the journey grew even more difficult. Poor grass to eat and rough roads took a toll on the oxen. The travelers also worried about being attacked.
Keep your eyes open.
We're on Indian land.
After crossing the Great Basin Desert, they had one last obstacle, the Sierra Nevada mountains.
Just think, son—
— all that gold is waiting for us just on the other side of those mountains.

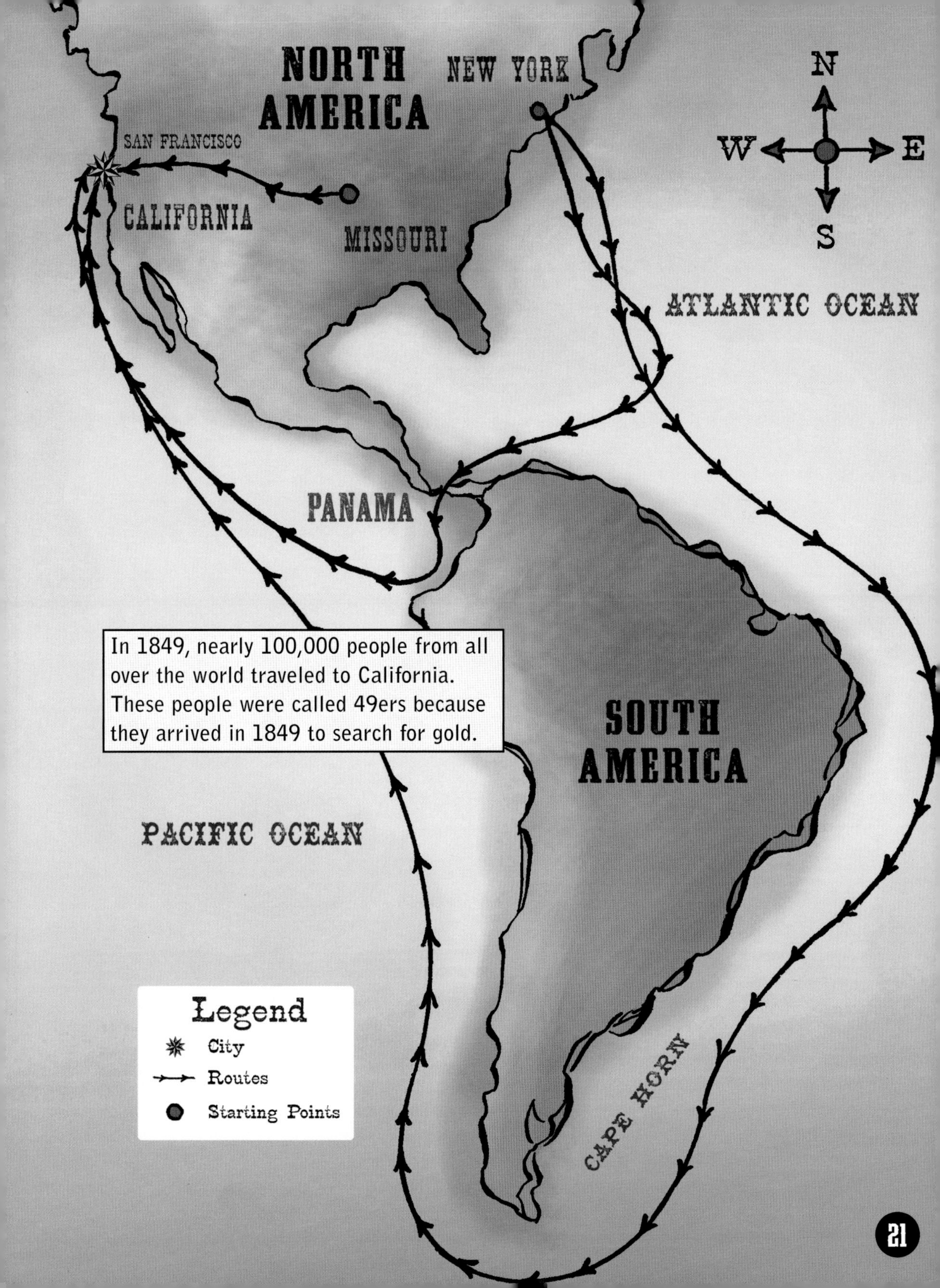
NORTH AMERICA
NEW YORK
SAN FRANCISCO
CALIFORNIA
MISSOURI
N
W
E
S
ATLANTIC OCEAN
PANAMA
SOUTH AMERICA
PACIFIC OCEAN
CAPE HORN
Legend
City
Routes
Starting Points

In 1849, nearly 100,000 people from all over the world traveled to California. These people were called 49ers because they arrived in 1849 to search for gold.

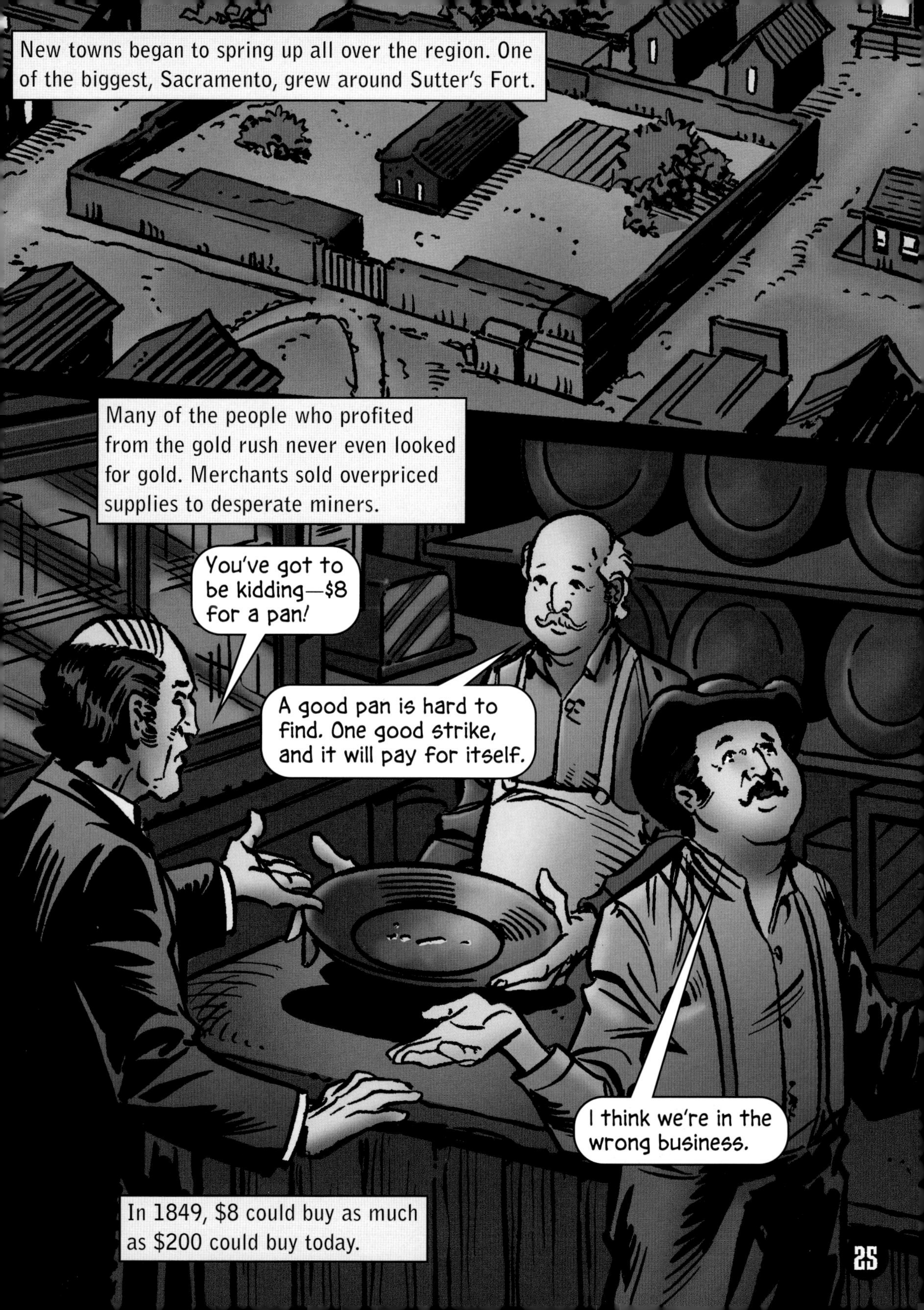
New towns began to spring up all over the region. One of the biggest, Sacramento, grew around Sutter's Fort.
Many of the people who profited from the gold rush never even looked for gold. Merchants sold overpriced supplies to desperate miners.
You've got to be kidding—$8 for a pan!
A good pan is hard to find. One good strike, and it will pay for itself.
I think we're in the wrong business.
In 1849, $8 could buy as much as $200 could buy today.

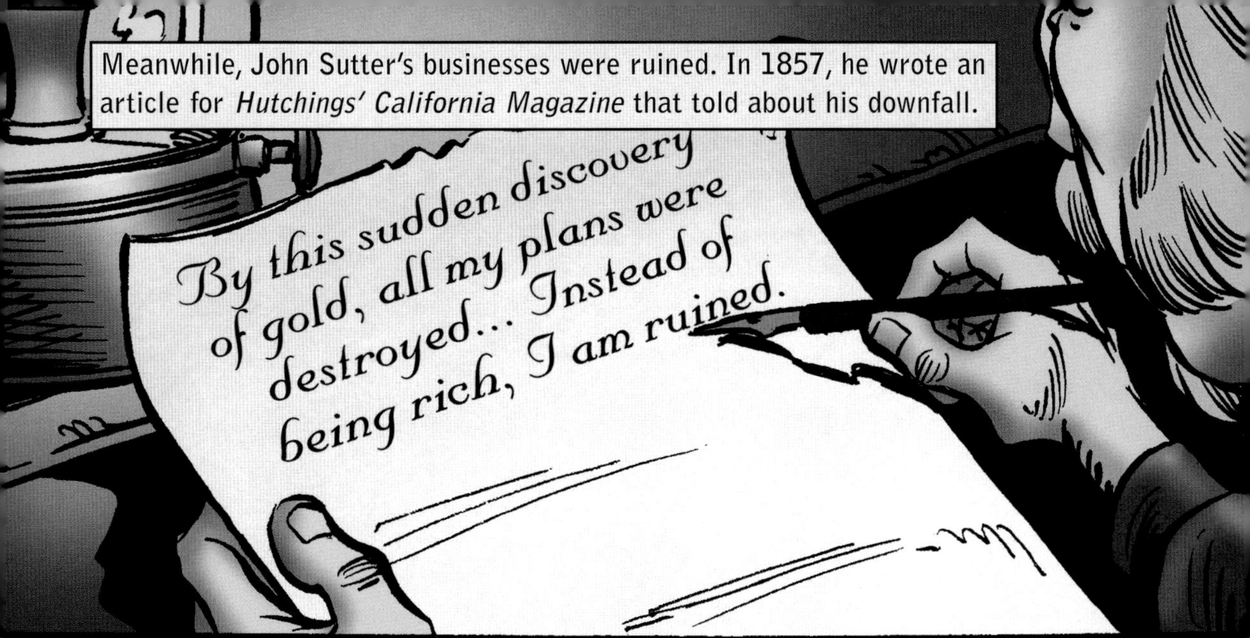
Meanwhile, John Sutter's businesses were ruined. In 1857, he wrote an article for *Hutchings' California Magazine* that told about his downfall.
By this sudden discovery of gold, all my plans were destroyed... Instead of being rich, I am ruined.

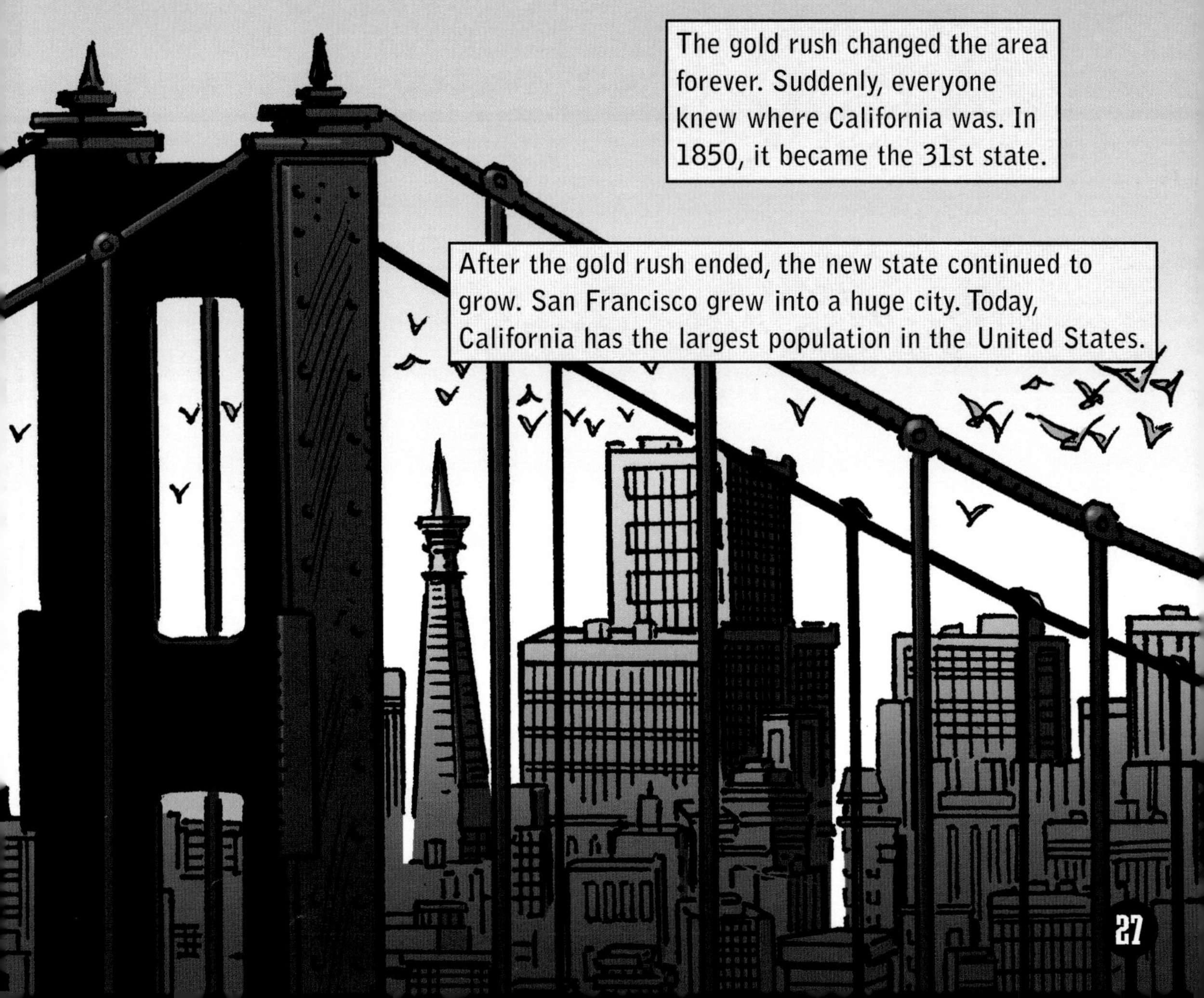
The gold rush changed the area forever. Suddenly, everyone knew where California was. In 1850, it became the 31st state.
After the gold rush ended, the new state continued to grow. San Francisco grew into a huge city. Today, California has the largest population in the United States.

MORE ABOUT THE ★ GOLD RUSH

- In January 1848, California was not yet a part of the United States. The United States had just defeated Mexico in the Mexican War (1846–1848). The two countries were working on a peace treaty that would give the territory of California to the United States. At the time, neither government knew about the gold. California was admitted as a state in 1850.

- Miners came to California from all over the world. Many early miners crossed the border from Mexico. People sailed from China to search for gold. Even people as far away as Europe came to California, dreaming of riches.

- About one out of 10 people who took the overland route to California died along the way. Cholera was one of the most common causes of death. Travelers got cholera from drinking polluted water.

- A woman named Margaret Frink made a fortune during the gold rush. But she never looked for gold. She cooked and sold food to hungry miners. She said she sold $18,000 worth of pies. That amount would be almost $400,000 in today's money.

- When the gold rush started, San Francisco had only about 500 people. At first, many people left town to search for their fortunes. But the town wasn't deserted for long. By 1849, so many people arrived in the area that more than 20,000 people lived in San Francisco.

- The discovery of gold was so important to California's development that today it is called the Golden State.

- During the gold rush, two men, Henry Wells and William Fargo, decided to start a bank for miners. Today, Wells Fargo is one of the largest banking companies in the world.

- In 1853, mining companies started using hydraulic mining. This destructive mining method used powerful jets of water to tear up land. The jets were so strong that they could kill a person from 200 feet (61 meters) away. Thirty years later, hydraulic mining was banned.

- Many small towns started as the 49ers rushed into California. After the gold rush was over, some of these towns were abandoned. They became ghost towns. Some ghost towns still stand today.

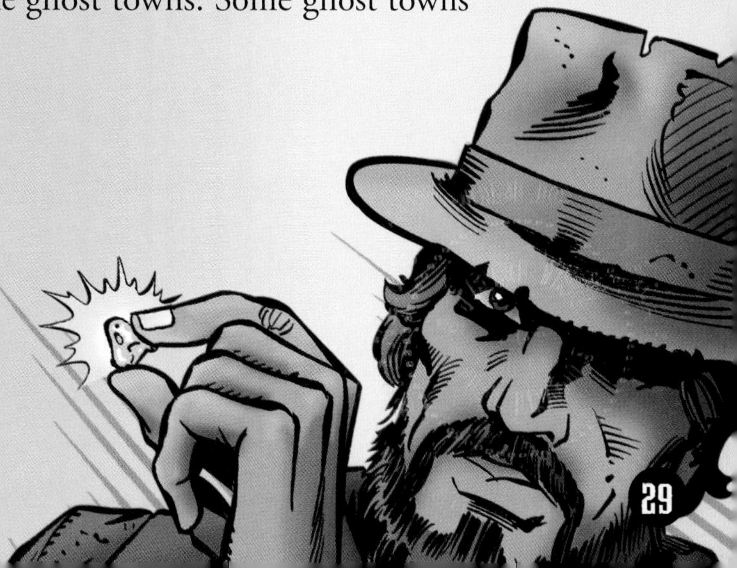

GLOSSARY

cholera (KOL-ur-uh)—a disease that causes severe sickness and diarrhea; the main cause of cholera during the gold rush was polluted water.

claim jumper (KLAYM JUHM-pur)—a person who steals land that belongs to someone else

malaria (muh-LAIR-ee-uh)—a tropical disease people get from mosquito bites; symptoms include chills, fever, and sweating.

millrace (MIL-rayss)—a trench that allows water to travel from a river to a mill

sawmill (SAW-mil)—a place where people use machines to saw logs into boards

INTERNET SITES

FactHound offers a safe, fun way to find Internet sites related to this book. All of the sites on FactHound have been researched by our staff.

Here's how:

1. *Visit www.facthound.com*
2. Type in this special code **0736843701** for age-appropriate sites. Or enter a search word related to this book for a more general search.
3. Click on the **Fetch It** button.

FactHound will fetch the best sites for you!

READ MORE

Blashfield, Jean F. *The California Gold Rush.* We the People. Minneapolis: Compass Point Books, 2001.

Crewe, Sabrina, and Michael V. Uschan. *The California Gold Rush.* Events That Shaped America. Milwaukee: Gareth Stevens, 2003.

Gregory, Kristiana. *Seeds of Hope: The Gold Rush Diary of Susanna Fairchild, California Territory, 1849.* Dear America. New York: Scholastic, 2001.

Hayhurst, Chris. *John Sutter: California Pioneer.* Primary Sources of Famous People in American History. New York: Rosen, 2004.

BIBLIOGRAPHY

All about the Gold Rush
http://www.isu.edu/~trinmich/allabout.html.

Boessenecker, John. *Gold Dust and Gunsmoke: Tales of Gold Rush Outlaws, Gunfighters, Lawmen, and Vigilantes.* New York: John Wiley, 1999.

Brands, H. W. *The Age of Gold: The California Gold Rush and the New American Dream.* New York: Doubleday, 2002.

Rau, Margaret. *The Wells Fargo Book of the Gold Rush.* New York: Atheneum, 2001.

INDEX